Quokkas

FIRST EDITION

US Senior Editor Shannon Beatty; **US Editor** Jane Perlmutter; **Senior Editor** Carrie Love;
Project Editor Kritika Gupta; **Art Editors** Mohd Zishan, Polly Appleton; **Jacket Co-Ordinator** Issy Walsh;
Jacket Designer Dheeraj Arora; **DTP Designers** Dheeraj Singh, Nand Kishore Acharya;
Project Picture Researcher Sakshi Saluja; **Producer, Pre-Production** Tony Phipps;
Senior Producer Ena Matagic; **Managing Editors** Penny Smith, Monica Saigal;
Deputy Managing Art Editor Ivy Sengupta; **Managing Art Editor** Mabel Chan;
Delhi Team Head Malavika Talukder; **Publishing Manager** Francesca Young;
Creative Director Helen Senior; **Publishing Director** Sarah Larter;
Reading Consultant Dr. Barbara Marinak; **Subject Consultant** Kim Bryan

THIS EDITION

Editorial Management by Oriel Square
Produced for DK by WonderLab Group LLC
Jennifer Emmett, Erica Green, Kate Hale, *Founders*

Editors Grace Hill Smith, Libby Romero, Maya Myers, Michaela Weglinski;
Photography Editors Kelley Miller, Annette Kiesow, Nicole DiMella; **Managing Editor** Rachel Houghton;
Designers Project Design Company; **Researcher** Michelle Harris; **Copy Editor** Lori Merritt;
Indexer Connie Binder; **Proofreader** Larry Shea; **Reading Specialist** Dr. Jennifer Albro;
Curriculum Specialist Elaine Larson

Published in the United States by DK Publishing
1745 Broadway, 20th Floor, New York, NY 10019

Copyright © 2023 Dorling Kindersley Limited
DK, a Division of Penguin Random House LLC
23 24 25 26 10 9 8 7 6 5 4 3 2 1
001-334076-July/2023

All rights reserved.

Without limiting the rights under the copyright reserved above, no part of this publication may be reproduced, stored in or introduced into a retrieval system, or transmitted, in any form, or by any means (electronic, mechanical, photocopying, recording, or otherwise), without the prior written permission of the copyright owner.
Published in Great Britain by Dorling Kindersley Limited

A catalog record for this book
is available from the Library of Congress.
HC ISBN: 978-0-7440-7402-4
PB ISBN: 978-0-7440-7403-1

DK books are available at special discounts when purchased in bulk for sales promotions, premiums, fundraising, or educational use. For details, contact: DK Publishing Special Markets,
1745 Broadway, 20th Floor, New York, NY 10019
SpecialSales@dk.com

Printed and bound in China

The publisher would like to thank the following for their kind permission to reproduce their images:
a=above; c=center; b=below; l=left; r=right; t=top; b/g=background

Dreamstime.com: SappheirosPhoto 1b; **Getty Images / iStock:** J_Knaupe 3a-6; **naturepl.com:** Joel Sartore / Photo Ark 3cb

Cover images: *Front:* **Dreamstime.com:** Oliverneumann; *Spine:* **Dreamstime.com:** Oliverneumann

All other images © Dorling Kindersley
For more information see: www.dkimages.com

For the curious
www.dk.com

Level 2

Quokkas

Caryn Jenner

Contents

6	Meet the Quokkas
12	Where Do Quokkas Live?
14	Growing Up
20	Cute Critters

26 Quokka Survival
30 Glossary
31 Index
32 Quiz

Meet the Quokkas

Look at these animals. Do you see the smiles on their furry faces?

These animals are quokkas. A quokka looks like it is smiling because the ends of its mouth turn up.

That's why quokkas are called the happiest animals in the world.

A quokka is about the size of a house cat.
It has a round, compact body with thick, brown fur.
Its tail is thin, like a rat's tail.

A quokka has big back paws and small front paws.
Watch out! It also has sharp claws.

Lightweight

Quokkas can weigh up to nine pounds (4 kg).

A female quokka has a special pouch on her tummy. This is where she keeps her baby.

A baby quokka is called a joey. See the little joey peeking out of its pouch?

A joey stays in its mother's pouch for up to six and a half months.

Marsupials

An animal that keeps its baby in a pouch is called a marsupial. Wallabies, kangaroos, koalas, and wombats are marsupials. A quokka is a kind of wallaby.

Quokka

Happy Birthday!

Quokkas usually have one baby at a time, but sometimes they have twins.

Red-necked wallaby

Red kangaroo

Where Do Quokkas Live?

Happy Home

Rottnest Island is home to about 10,000 quokkas.

Quokkas live in Australia. Most quokkas live on Rottnest Island off the coast of Australia.

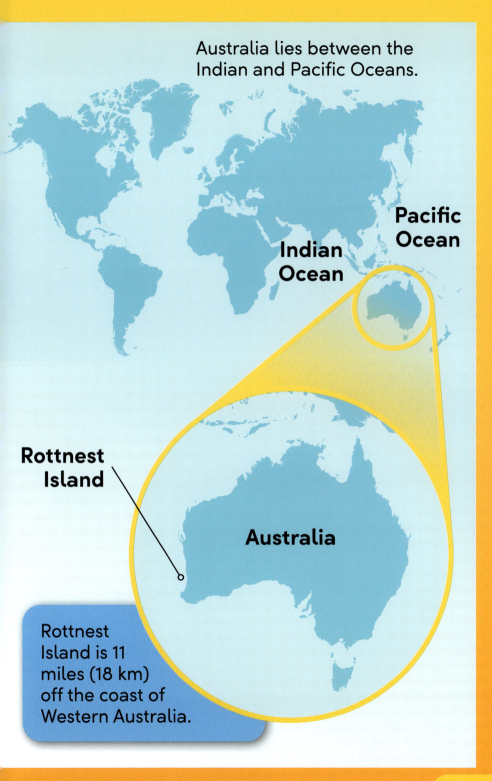

Growing Up

A newborn quokka joey is only about the size of a raisin. The tiny joey stays safe and warm in its mother's pouch.

It feeds on its mother's milk. It doesn't look like a quokka until it gets older.

A young joey inside its mother's pouch

A joey peeks out of its mother's pouch.

Soon the quokka joey grows fur. It pokes its head out of its mother's pouch and looks around.

After about six months, the joey climbs out of the pouch for the first time.
It's ready to explore!

After about eight months, the quokka joey grows too big for its mother's pouch. It can find its own food.

A quokka mother and baby on Rottnest Island, Australia

Soon it will be all grown up.
It may stay with its mother until
it is about 20 months old.

Cute Critters

Hop, hop, hop! Quokkas hop around on their big back paws. Sometimes, they move around on all four paws.

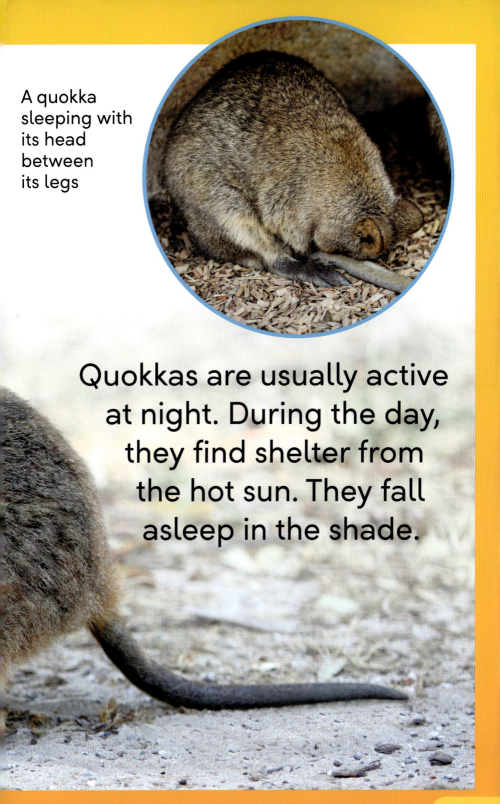

A quokka sleeping with its head between its legs

Quokkas are usually active at night. During the day, they find shelter from the hot sun. They fall asleep in the shade.

Quokkas eat grass
and leaves, and stems
of shrubs and bushes.
They climb up small
bushes and trees.
They pull down the branches
with their sharp claws
and eat the leaves.

Sometimes, there is no food.
Then the quokka gets energy
from fat stored in its tail.

Hiding Out

Quokkas spend most of their time in bushes and undergrowth.

23

Quokkas live near streams and swamps.
They drink the water.
They also get water from the plants they eat.

Sometimes, quokkas make trails to help them get from place to place.

A quokka jumps across a stream.

Quokka Survival

People come to Rottnest Island especially to see the popular quokkas.

Since quokkas are wild, people are not allowed to touch them or feed them.

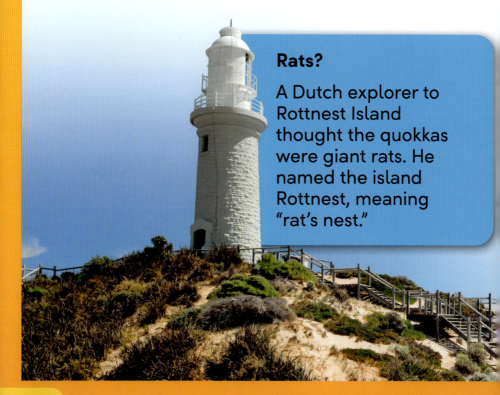

Rats?

A Dutch explorer to Rottnest Island thought the quokkas were giant rats. He named the island Rottnest, meaning "rat's nest."

Deforestation

Quokkas have lost much of their habitat on mainland Australia due to wildfires and deforestation.

There used to be a lot of quokkas on mainland Australia, too.
Sadly, there aren't many left there now.
Animals such as foxes and cats hunt them.
People build roads and buildings on the quokkas' habitat and destroy it.
Large wildfires also destroy the quokkas' habitat.

An orphaned quokka joey in Australia

People in Australia are trying to protect the quokkas' habitat so it doesn't completely disappear.

Hopefully, the quokkas will keep smiling for a long time to come.

Glossary

Deforestation
Cutting down trees over a large area

Habitat
Where an animal or plant lives

Mammal
A warm-blooded animal that produces milk to feed its young

Marsupial
A type of mammal. Most female marsupials have a pouch in which their young live.

Native
Relating to an animal or plant that occurs naturally in a place

Swamp
Low-lying wet ground also known as a bog

Index

Australia 12, 13, 18, 27–28
claws 9, 22
deforestation 27
eating 22, 24
fur 8, 16
habitat 27–28
hiding 22
joey 10, 14–19, 28
kangaroos 10, 11

koalas 10
leaves 22
marsupials 10
mouth 6
paws 9, 20
pouch 10, 14–18
red kangaroo 11
red-necked wallaby 11
Rottnest Island 12, 13, 18, 26

size 9, 14
sleeping 21
smiling 6
survival 26–28
tail 9, 22
wallabies 10, 11

Quiz

Answer the questions to see what you have learned. Check your answers in the key below.

1. Why does a quokka look like it's smiling?
2. How much does a quokka weigh?
3. What is a joey?
4. Where does a female quokka keep her baby?
5. Where do quokkas live?

1. The ends of its mouth turn up 2. Up to nine lbs (4 kg)
3. A baby marsupial 4. In a special pouch on her tummy
5. In Australia, mostly on Rottnest Island